The British Museum

nosy crow

so YOU THINK YOU'VE GOT IT BAD?

A KID'S LIFE IN ANCIENT ROME

D1287181

First published 2019 by Nosy Crow Ltd
The Crow's Nest, 14 Baden Place,
Crosby Row, London SE1 1YW
www.nosycrow.com

ISBN 978 1 78800 475 6 (HB)
ISBN 978 1 78800 706 1 (PB)

Nosy Crow and associated logos are trademarks
and/or registered trademarks of Nosy Crow Ltd.

Published in collaboration with the British Museum.

Text © Chae Strathie 2019
Illustrations © Marisa Morea 2019

The right of Chae Strathie to be identified as the author and Marisa Morea
to be identified as the illustrator of this work has been asserted.

All rights reserved.

This book is sold subject to the condition that it shall not,
by way of trade or otherwise, be lent, hired out or otherwise circulated in
any form of binding or cover other than that in which it is published.
No part of this publication may be reproduced, stored in a retrieval system,
or transmitted in any form or by any means
(electronic, mechanical, photocopying, recording or otherwise)
without the prior written permission of Nosy Crow Ltd.

A CIP catalogue record for this book is available from the British Library.

Printed in China.
Papers used by Nosy Crow are made from wood
grown in sustainable forests.

1 3 5 7 9 8 6 4 2 (HB)
3 5 7 9 8 6 4 2 (PB)

SO *YOU* THINK **YOU'VE** *GOT IT* **BAD?**

A KID'S LIFE IN **ANCIENT ROME**

CONTENTS

CLOTHES AND HAIRSTYLES

You know what it's like. All you want to do is leave the house so you can get to that new zombie-themed ice cream parlour – the one that does BRAIN SUNDAES – but Mum and Dad are taking aaaaaaaaaaaaaaages getting ready.

Mum's spent roughly **FIVE YEARS** so far putting her make-up on, while Dad's making sure his "cool" new jacket is zipped-up *just* right and his hair is brushed at a special angle so it hides that **SHINY BALD BIT** on top of his noggin.

It's a **MAHOOSIVE** pain in the bottom waiting for grown-ups to get ready . . . but if **YOU THINK** *YOU'VE* **GOT IT BAD**, just say a big-old "thanks bro" that you weren't kicking around in the days of ancient Rome.

> Mmmm, this soup is delicious – though it does taste a little snaily.

> Has anyone seen my bowl of disgusting face cream?

Back then, your parents could have taken a lot longer to get their hair styled perfectly, and your mum's make-up might have left you reaching for a **SICK BUCKET**!

For instance, bear fat was used to make hair grow, while a mixture made from **ANTS' EGGS** was used to blacken women's eyebrows. Some people even used a lovely face cream made from – wait for it – **SQUISHED SUN-DRIED SNAILS** mixed into a bean broth! If you think that's bad, at least **SNAIL FACE CREAM** couldn't kill you. Many other face creams contained lead, a type of poisonous metal that can build up in the body over time causing brain damage and even death!

A Roman woman's hair was very important to her. So much so that special enslaved people were trained to look after their mistresses' lovely locks. And if a woman didn't have enough hairy stuff on her headbox for her liking, she could simply pop a **BIG WIG** on.

These allowed women to achieve the super-tall styles that were popular during certain periods in ancient Rome. The writer Juvenal even compared them to multistorey buildings! Imagine how long it would take your mum to build a **SKYSCRAPER** on her head.

FANCY THAT!

Roman emperors didn't want to be thought of as kings, so they didn't wear golden crowns. Instead, they popped laurel wreaths on their heads to symbolize their success and power. Why not try wrapping some twigs round your coconut and telling your pals that you're SUPER-POWERFUL?

Hmm . . . I'm gonna need a bigger wig . . .

7

Your dad might slap some hair gel on, but at least he doesn't sprinkle GOLD DUST on his thatch, which is what the Emperor Lucius Verus did to make himself appear blonder than he actually was.

Very nice until it rained – then it was bye-bye golden hair, hello golden FACE.

EMPEROR LUCIUS VERUS

My hair looks amazing!

Yeah, but it smells like poop!

And if your dad is a bit funny about going grey, nowadays he just has to dye his hair. But back in ancient Rome, some people wore a paste on their heads at night that was made from ground herbs and EARTHWORMS to keep the grey away!

If you think that sounds bad, PIGEON POOP was used to lighten hair, and to dye hair black the writer Pliny the Elder reckoned rubbing in LEECHES that had been rotted in red wine for 40 days was the way to go!

Oh, and if you have a little case of head lice (nothing to be ashamed of – happens to lots of peeps), while some (sensible) ancient Romans used lice combs, others used GOAT DUNG to combat the annoying little beasties instead!

What about clothing? Are you bored with your togs? Fed up with that tracksuit? Sick of the sight of your hoodie? Had it up to here with the same old t-shirt?

Well, at least you **HAVE** clothes to choose from.

Back in ancient Rome it was pretty much toga-land as far as the eye could see. Your choice was basically a toga or a tunic. Or perhaps a tunic or a toga, if you were feeling particularly funky.

TUNIC

TOGA

Most Roman clothing was made of wool or linen, although rich folk also had access to **EXPENSIVE** silk from China or high-quality Egyptian cotton. Many Roman clothes could be quite colourful, although purple clothes were only for the super-important or super-rich. The expensive purple dye was made by crushing the shells of thousands of Murex **SEA SNAILS**.

You're totally going to play with this, aren't you?

MUREX SEA SNAIL

Girls wore a long tunic that reached their feet, while boys wore a shorter tunic, sometimes with stripy socks.

The most important day in a boy's life was when he was given his *toga virilis*, which marked his transition from childhood to being a man. He would give up all his childhood toys at the same time.

That's like hitting your teens and getting a new pair of grown-up tweed trousers but having to bin your games console and skateboard. Sounds **AWFUL!**

FAMILY LIFE

Grown-ups sometimes have pretty weird ideas about what makes a family home look all swanky and stylish, don't they?

They might pop a crazy painting on the wall featuring a few yellow squiggles and a green blob that looks like someone has done a **MEGA-SNEEZE** on the canvas, then they'll stand back, rub their chin and go: "Hmmm, yah, simply **SUPERB** modern art."

Or maybe they'll try some **DIY** art themselves by gluing a twig and a sock to an empty milk carton and spraying it all gold. Hey presto! A magnificent sculpture!

Yeah, whatever you say, Dad.

FANCY THAT!

In the home of the first Roman emperor, Augustus, 18 enslaved people were employed to make and repair clothes. You probably don't have ANY servants just waiting to fix that hole in the toe of your superhero socks or make you a shiny new pair of pants when your old ones wear out. Poor you!

And *this* is my great uncle Maximus!

But while that may well be embarrassing when you bring your pals home from school, if you think you've got it bad, at least you don't have **DEAD ANCESTORS** peering down at you from the walls.

Yes, family was such a big deal to the Romans that in some cases they would make wax moulds of relatives who'd popped their clogs to create "**DEATH MASKS**" that they could put up on the walls of their home.

Most families would also regularly go to the graves of their ancestors to pay their respects to the dead. So next time you feel like launching into a **GRUMBLEFEST** about going shopping for school trousers, just remember you could be going on a fun day out to a cemetery.

Hey Atticus – did you hear that my dead ancestor had to go to the doctor?

He was COFFIN all the time!

Really Flavia? What was wrong with him?

Lol.

Do you ever wish . . .
you didn't have to do laundry?

Don't you just hate tidying your bedroom? It's just SOOOO hard picking up your stinky old clothes off the floor and getting them into the laundry basket. Luckily, the next stop for your whiffy socks and pants is a washing machine, and not an ancient Roman laundry.

Roman clothes were usually washed at laundries where they were placed in large tubs containing old urine (yup, that's wee we're talking about), then squished underfoot by bare-footed workers.

White clothes could be brightened even more by treating them with sulphur fumes, which stink of rotten eggs. So your threads would be lovely and clean . . . but you'd stink of wee and eggy bottom burps. Excellent!

Aside from being stared at by masks of dead relatives, what else did kids in Roman families get up to? In most cases, it was whatever their dad told them to do . . .

The thing is, if your dad decided you had to do something, you SERIOUSLY had to do it. That's because the oldest male of the household – which was usually the father – had COMPLETE POWER over the family.

He was known as the *paterfamilias* and he decided EVERYTHING. He could even arrange the marriages of his family members . . . and for girls that could be at a young age.

The paterfamilias (why not try calling your dad that from now on?) could be a very strict keeper of discipline. Physical punishments could be imposed for being CHEEKY, bad behaviour or any kind of disobedience – even for poor schoolwork.

Even more extreme, when a new baby was born it would be laid at its father's feet – if the father picked the baby up it would become part of the family, but if he ignored the baby it would be abandoned, possibly to be raised by a childless family, but more likely to be raised as an enslaved person.

PHEW...

Hey girls! Looking forward to hanging out with your pals and doing all sorts of cool stuff when you're 14? Well think again. In ancient Rome you could have to give up your childhood things and say hello to a hubby (who would be years older). **NO. THANK. YOU.**

Women and girls had a particularly tough time – well there's a surprise. Sons were seen as being much more important than daughters, which we know is as silly as a swimming pool full of clowns, but that's what the ancient peeps thought. Even worse, a man could **DIVORCE** his wife if she kept giving him baby girls instead of a son . . . as if she **HAD A CHOICE!**

Women and girls were also expected to run the home, cook, clean and raise the children. Many mums died young, either because having babies in those days could be pretty dangerous, or as a result of disease.

FANCY THAT!

It's believed many poor children were first sent to work by their family between the ages of five and 10. One child was recorded as saying: "Today . . . I am seven years old, and must play no more. Here is my top, my hoop and my ball: keep them all." So stop fiddling with that app and GET TO WORK!

13

Just to keep the whole "aren't we having fun" levels running high, the Roman day lasted from dawn till dusk.

So you and your family were out of bed super-early and, unless you were rich enough to afford oil for lamps, you all went to bed when it got dark. Or stayed up and played hilarious games of "Try to Avoid Stepping in the Chamber Pot or Falling Down the Stairs".

That said, there were some upsides to Roman family life. The ancient Romans loved animals (although they also loved killing animals for sport – and when we say animals we're not talking about wasps or fleas. We mean big furry ones, which is pretty mean).

HEE HEE!

BIRD

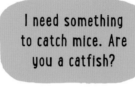

I need something to catch mice. Are you a catfish?

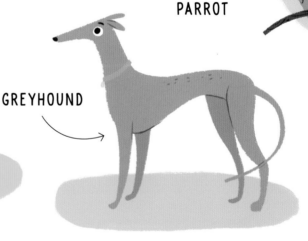

PARROT

GREYHOUND

MONKEY

If you were lucky enough, you might have had a pet or two around the house. Typical pets included greyhounds, ferrets, parrots and other birds, fish, and even small **MONKEYS!** You may think your little brother is a small monkey, but that's not the same thing. He's hopefully slightly less hairy for a start!

MALTESE

One of the most commonly owned pets was a small white dog with long hair called a Maltese (not to be confused with a Malteser, which would be a very weird pet and rubbish at chasing sticks). Much like today, dogs wore tags in case they got lost, and bigger, fiercer dogs were used as guard dogs to protect people's homes.

Cats however, were not popular pets, and Romans kept ferrets to hunt mice and rats instead.

FERRET

FANCY THAT!
Unfortunately for many Roman pets, some of them were considered a bit too DELICIOUS by their owners, so a pet bird or fish might end up in the cooking pot. PARROTS' TONGUES were considered a particularly tasty delicacy. BLEUGH!

Have you seen Polly? I'm sure she was in her cage earlier.

Um . . . no?

Squawk!

Do you ever wish . . . your parents didn't make you do boring chores?

Is there anything worse than having to do the vacuuming to earn your pocket money? Anything? Anything at all? No way – there simply can't be!

Unless you count being an enslaved person in ancient Rome (or in any other time or place for that matter). That's worse.

Some children in ancient Rome were enslaved and could be treated badly. They had to work extremely long hours, from sunrise to sunset, doing jobs like serving wine or food at their master's table or carrying out hard farm work. They could even be used as actors and dancers!

Rich families had many enslaved people to cook, clean and do the gardening. There were even cases of poor people selling their children to richer neighbours as enslaved people when times were tough.

Although many enslaved people were treated very badly, it wasn't always the case. Some families became fond of their enslaved people and freed them. Once freed, a *"freedman"* took their master's name and could even become a Roman citizen, and some of them went on to become very rich and powerful.

Still, the vacuuming seems a better bet all round, don't you think?

THE HOME

How messy an eater are you? Let's do a quick test to find out! You have a BURGER and a BANANA MILKSHAKE, do you . . .

A) Consume them gracefully with not a crumb or drop spilt.

B) Dribble a little ketchup down your chin and end up with a **SPLAT** of yellow milkshake on your nice white t-shirt.

C) Squeeze the cup so hard it **EXPLODES** and covers your entire head in banana gunk – then miss your mouth completely while eating the burger and **RAM IT UP YOUR NOSE** – before dropping the greasy remains all over your expensive new trainers.

WHOOPS

So how did you do? If you answered:

A) Congratulations! You are a normally-functioning human being.

B) Could try harder. Have a go at closing your mouth occasionally.

C) Oh dear. Oh deary, deary dear. You should consider wearing an all-over plastic bodysuit while eating and getting **HOSED DOWN** afterwards.

But if you think transferring food successfully into your mouth is difficult, at least you have the option of eating sitting upright. In ancient Rome they often ate **LYING DOWN!**

During dinner in a rich person's house, everyone would lie across large couches, while enslaved people brought them food and wine. Sound **MESSY?**

Well, add to that the fact that people ate with their hands, and it's no wonder people had to clean themselves with perfumed water between courses.

HELLO?

The dining room – or *triclinium* – was one of the most important rooms in the ancient Roman home. In fact, some really posh homes might have had up to **FOUR** dining rooms. They would be decorated with murals on the walls and expensive mosaics made of thousands of tiny squares of marble, glass, pottery, tile, shell or stone on the floor. You can recreate this look by drawing a lovely picture in felt tip on your dining room walls and arranging gravel in a pretty pattern on the floor. Your parents are going to be **SOOO** pleased.

Guests would be seated (or rather, be sent to **LIE DOWN**) on couches in order of importance, with the couches arranged in a U-shape around the table. The most important guests were always in the middle and the least important were the furthest from the hosts on the far side of the table. If you were on a small stool in another room altogether, the host **REALLY** didn't like you.

So what would the inside of a rich Roman's home look like? Let's step inside this *domus* — or town house — and see . . .

The front door usually opened into a central hall or *atrium* which had an open roof and a pool in the middle of the floor. Paddling in it with SMELLY FEET was generally frowned upon.

Most homes had their own shrine called a *lararium*, where household gods called lares were worshipped. This was a sacred place where the family made offerings. The family could choose any gods to worship, although two favourites were Vesta, the goddess of the home, and Janus, the god of doors and time, which sounds like he got a bit of a poor deal when the god jobs were being handed out . . .

LARARIUM

Some well-off Romans would have also had their own bathrooms or *lavatrina* with built-in toilets and a pool or basin to wash in, however many people still went to the public bath houses to wash. Imagine not having a shower at home and popping to the swimming baths with a BAR OF SOAP instead. Embarrassing or what?

There would also have been several bedrooms and an office, as well as a walled courtyard garden called a *peristylium* where the family could relax in the sunshine surrounded by plants, sculptures and fountains.

ATRIUM

KITCHEN

HYPOCAUST

FANCY THAT!

If you were to search the archaeological remains of a Roman domus or villa looking for the enslaved people's rooms, you'd find it hard. Enslaved people often slept in the DOORWAY of their master's bedroom! So if you think your room is small, count yourself lucky that you HAVE a bedroom.

Rich Romans would also have had a kitchen, although they wouldn't even make a **CHEESE SANDWICH** themselves as they had enslaved people to do all the housework, gardening and cooking. If you fancied a **PARROT TONGUE KEBAB**, all you had to do was holler!

Amazingly, some rich people's homes had a kind of **FANCY-PANTS** underfloor heating called *hypocaust*, where the floor was raised up on pillars so warm air could flow underneath. They even had access to sewers and running water. That's five-star living right there!

19

While a rich Roman family might have had a large town house and a luxurious country villa, the less well-off weren't quite so lucky . . .

Rome was a massive city for its time, with over a million inhabitants. Most middle-class and poorer people lived in tall blocks of flats called *insulae*, with shops and workspaces on the ground floor and apartments above.

People who were better off lived on the lower floors in large apartments, and the poorest people lived on the very top floors, sometimes in **DREADFUL** conditions.

Each *insula* could be horribly overcrowded, sometimes with entire families living in one room. And let's face it, it's sometimes bad enough living on the same **PLANET** as your annoying brother or sister, let alone the same room!

There were rarely proper toilets in these buildings, and as the upper storeys were often made of wood, they were in danger of catching fire. Even though it was against the law to build more than 18 metres high (about six storeys), some greedy landlords ignored these rules and built towers up to nine storeys high – that would often collapse!

FANCY THAT!

Although the ancient Romans had finally got around to inventing proper toilets, chamber pots were still the most common way to go to the loo. The famous Roman general Mark Antony was criticized for using a GOLD CHAMBER POT. So if you have a diamond encrusted loo, best keep quiet about it!

Do you ever wish . . . people shared things more?

Of course, sharing is a lovely idea – what's mine is yours and what's yours is mine, and all that jazz. It should be encouraged at all times. Well, maybe not all times . . .

You see, the ancient Romans used sponges on sticks instead of toilet paper . . . and in public toilets these were shared!

Still think sharing is the bee's knees? Thought not.

Speaking of sharing, public latrines could be huge and open-plan with up to 25 seats. Some could even hold as many as 80 people. Imagine the smell! Anyone want a clothes peg?

Almost all the houses that have been excavated in the Roman towns of Herculaneum and Pompeii had toilets, although some were in the kitchen and there is no evidence they had doors.

At least you could wave to your family while they were at the dinner table. "Yoo-hoo!" Or should that be "you-poo"?

Eww! No thanks!

EDUCATION

Some people simply don't "get" numbers. In school they're WONDERFUL with words, PERFECT with pictures and SUPERB with sounds.

But when faced with numbers in class, they scream, shout "wibble-wibble-**PANCAKE!**" and run into the playground with their jumper pulled over their head.

Perhaps you're one of those people? But if you think you've got it bad, imagine trying to add, subtract and do – gasp – **LONG DIVISION** if numbers were letters!

That's one of the things Roman kids had to get their ancient brainboxes round in school.

Unlike the Arabic numbers we use today (1, 2, 3 etc. You know the drill), Roman numerals were represented by letters (also known as symbols). Now for the tricky bit:

When a symbol appears **AFTER** a larger (or equal) symbol, you add them together. But if the symbol appears **BEFORE** a larger symbol, it is subtracted.

So, for 3 you would write III; for 7 you would write VII; for 14 you would write XIV (that's 10 plus 5 minus 1 – do keep up . . . and stop picking your nose at the back of the class).

If you wanted to write 78 you'd have to put down LXXVIII! And so on.

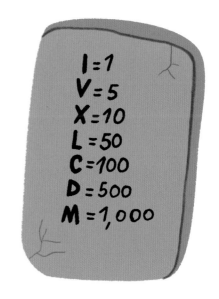

I = 1
V = 5
X = 10
L = 50
C = 100
D = 500
M = 1,000

Once you get into the **REALLY BIG** numbers, you're practically writing a **BOOK!**

Here are some Roman numerals – can you work out what numbers they represent?

A: CXI   B: MCCXXXIV   C: MMMCMLXXVIII

FANCY THAT!
Imagine you had to trundle along bumpy, muddy tracks whenever you were being driven anywhere. You'd spill your chocolate milkshake all over your funny little face. Before the Romans arrived, countries like Britain had no real roads. The Romans built new-fangled straight, flat roads all over the shop. In fact, they created more than 16,000 km (10,000 miles) of them! It was a Roman road-fest!

Do you ever wish . . . you could boss loads of people around?

Well, if you were in charge of the Roman Empire at its height you'd have to boss 70 million people around. That's some serious bossing right there, chum.

It was one of the largest empires in history, with the Roman army conquering huge areas of other countries, such as France and Britain.

To cover so much ground it had to move quickly – its soldiers could march up to 40 kilometres (25 miles) a day! Not impressed? You try doing that while carrying a sword, spear, shield, armour and other equipment! They didn't even have scooters or roller blades to help them get around.

The furthest north the Romans got was Britain. Around 2,000 years ago, Britain was ruled by tribes of people called the Celts . . . but they were in for a nasty shock. In AD 43, the mighty Roman army invaded the south of England and conquered most of the country.

They didn't do so well once they reached Scotland, however. It was still controlled by fierce warrior tribes, who didn't give in to the invaders. In the end the Romans built huge walls, such as Hadrian's Wall in the north of England, to keep the scary folk out.

So, if you ever bump into a Roman soldier and you want to give him a fright, just put on a Scottish accent and do the Highland Fling and he'll run a mile!

The Romans were also very big on other types of lessons. Pupils would study Latin — a form of which was spoken in ancient Rome — Greek, philosophy and rhetoric (the art of public speaking).

Does that sound much like the lessons you get in school? Didn't think so. And before you ask, "the art of public speaking" does not mean having a **CHINWAG** with your buddy in class when you should be concentrating on what the teacher is saying!

Oh no! We've got double rhetoric from X o'clock until XII o'clock!

Urgh! I HATE rhetoric.

At least you get to go to school!

Boys from rich families were the only ones likely to get a proper education. Girls were educated up to primary age, but then had to learn household skills from their mothers. Poor people often couldn't read or write and were put to work at an early age.

FANCY THAT!
Roman books consisted of one or more papyrus scrolls rather than the books with pages we have today. The finest books were written on *vellum*, which is made from sheets of wafer thin animal skin, usually baby goat or lamb. And that is why to this day you NEVER see goats or lambs reading books!

24

Of course, back in those days the Romans didn't have computers in class to help them learn. But they did have **TABLETS!**

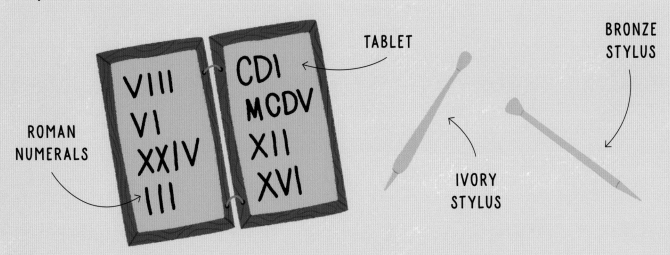

ROMAN NUMERALS

TABLET

BRONZE STYLUS

IVORY STYLUS

Before you go around telling people the Romans were totally clued up on apps and could play *Minecraft* around town, we're not talking about that kind of tablet. These were blocks of wood with shallow cavities carved in them, into which melted beeswax was poured to form a writing surface. Once you'd written on it with a sharpened metal "pen" called a *stylus* you could simply rub out the writing and use the tablet again. And it never needed to be charged up either!

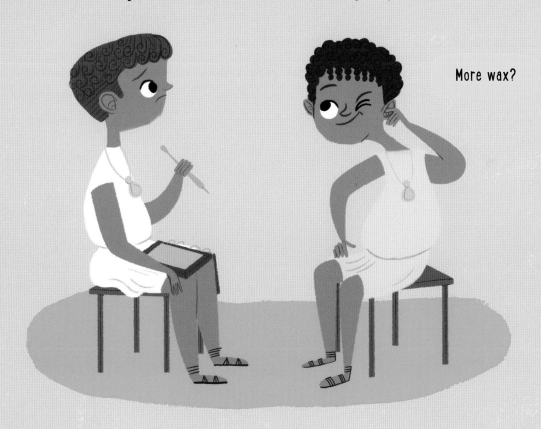

More wax?

Also, if you ran low on wax, you could always have a little noodle around in your **EARHOLE** for some emergency gunk to top it up.

So, if you're a hi-tech sort who prefers a screen you can **SWIPE** instead of a waxy blob you can **WIPE**, perhaps you wouldn't get on so well in ancient Rome . . .

Have you ever had your phone confiscated for ABSOLUTELY NO REASON when your ringtone went off in class?

Or had to pick up litter in the playground because there was a **REALLY IMPORTANT** piece of goss you **UTTERLY, POSITIVELY HAD** to share with your mate that just **COULDN'T WAIT** until after assembly?

Well if you think you've got it bad, the main way that teachers in ancient Rome used to discipline their students was using **FEAR** and **VIOLENCE**.

Those guys sound like a right old **BARREL OF LOLS.**

NOT!

SCARY TEACHER

The ancient Romans believed that boys would only learn accurately and correctly if they were **TERRIFIED** of being caned if they got things wrong. For boys who got things wrong **A LOT**, some schools would even bring in two enslaved people to hold the boys down while the teacher beat them with a leather whip! **OUCH!** It's enough to make your bottom jump off and run away and hide!

Even worse, boys had to go to school **SEVEN DAYS A WEEK**. No weekends! No lie-ins. Nothing. Although luckily, there were a lot of religious holidays, and students got some time off in the summer when the weather was hot. Still, **SEVEN** days a week of school, eh? It's just as well that idea didn't catch on!

Titus, this is the last warning! You're LATE for schoool!

But Muuuum, it's Sunday!

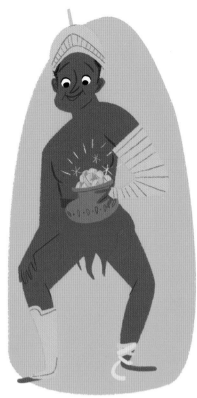

FANCY THAT!

In the late 2nd century AD, a decree (a ruling by the emperor) meant that gladiators who won their fights could be given a bonus payment of 500 *sestertii* – which was the amount a teacher might make in a whole year. Mind you, teachers had far less chance of being PRONGED by a big fork or eaten by a lion – even in REALLY NAUGHTY classes.

Do you ever wish . . . your family car was a bit more unusual?

Cars all look roughly the same, don't they? They're made of metal, have rubber wheels, an engine, a steering wheel. You know the rest. But what about something more . . . unique?

Well, you could try some Roman transport.

In ancient Roman times, people might travel in a *raeda*, a carriage that was their version of a mini-bus. It had wooden benches, clattering iron-covered wheels and a cloth roof – if it had a roof at all! It was pulled by horses or mules.

But don't bother jumping on board if you want to get anywhere fast – a journey that takes a couple of hours today would take more like six days back then!

If you were rich you might travel in a *carpentum*, which was more comfy but just as slow. Or if you were ultra-posh you could be carried around town by enslaved people on a *litter*, which was sort of like a mobile bed.

Why not ask your pals to lug you to school on a mattress – the perfect modern alternative!

27

GLADIATORS

It's great fun going to watch sport, isn't it? All that action, excitement and NAIL-BITING TENSION.

But there are some downsides. Sometimes the weather can be bad, so you get a bit cold and wet. And if the pitch is soggy and you're close to the action you might even end up splattered with MUD.

Mind you, if you had a choice between getting a blob of mud on your jacket or a blob of BRAINS, you'd probably go for the brown stuff. Unless you're SERIOUSLY weird!

Yes, if you think you've got it bad at mucky matches, at least they're MUDDY and not BLOODY, unlike the favourite entertainment of the ancient Romans.

Back in those days, gladiator battles were all the rage. And while a pulled muscle these days might see a sportsperson stretchered off the pitch, in those times the worst outcome might see you SKEWERED LIKE A KEBAB, which is never good for LOLs.

Gladiators were often enslaved people or criminals and were very well trained in gladiator schools, although free men and more rarely, women (yup, being a gladiator was an equal-opportunities sport in ancient Rome) often joined up, too. They would fight to the **DEATH** for the entertainment of the Roman public, from the very wealthiest to the poorest.

They battled it out in vast arenas called *amphitheatres*. The Colosseum in Rome is the greatest of them all.

It was opened by the Emperor Titus in AD 80 and could hold a whopping 50,000 people. A huge canvas covering was often stretched over the top to provide shade from the sun and a **MASSIVE** iron chandelier was dangled above the arena for night-time shows.

The floor was covered in sand . . . but not so the gladiators could build jolly **SANDCASTLES** when they were bored between getting all stabby – it was to soak up all the **BLOOD AND GORE**. Yeuch!

FANCY THAT!

Many people think that the Roman crowds put their thumbs down if they wanted a gladiator to be executed once he was beaten in a fight. But some experts think they actually put their thumbs UP to signal death. While we may never know the truth, next time you give a pal a cheerful thumbs up, just make sure there are no gladiators hanging about nearby or it could end BADLY for your chum.

While some gladiators fought each other, some fought **WILD ANIMALS** from across the Roman Empire.

Ferocious creatures such as **BEARS, LEOPARDS, BLACK PANTHERS** and **LIONS** were used. The **HAMSTER FIGHTS** were stopped due to lack of interest and the goldfish bouts never really took off either.

Keeping the crowds entertained was important and, just in case they got fed up with everyday killing, the floor of the Colosseum could be flooded and gladiators fought battles in little ships!

30

Even children could be brought in to fight on special occasions, although thankfully this was rare. Children saw gladiators and charioteers as **HEROES** in much the same way that sports stars are heroes for today's children. The fights may have been **GRUESOME** and **BLOODTHIRSTY** but interest in them was encouraged from a young age – a terracotta baby's bottle found in the ancient Roman town of Pompeii is decorated with the figure of a gladiator. What next? A sword instead of a rattle?

So while you might enjoy playing sports in school, just think yourself lucky that most of them don't end up with you as a **LEOPARD'S LUNCH**.

FANCY THAT!

When a person started at gladiator training school (voluntarily or not), they had to make a vow to allow themselves to be burned, whipped and killed with steel (GULP!), and gave up the rights to their life. They became the property of their schoolmaster, although they did get to keep most of the money they earned in fights and could become very rich.

Maximus! Can I get your autograph?

Are you a hopscotch ace? Do you excel at noughts and crosses? Is there no one who can come close to beating you at snakes and ladders?

Maybe you are the greatest at these . . . but you still hanker for a teensy bit more excitement? Then become a **ROMAN GLADIATOR!**

First you'll have to choose which kind of warrior to become. Here are your options:

THRAEX (The Thracian)

Carried a small square or rectangular shield. Main weapon was a short, curved sword or dagger called a *sica*. And you'd definitely be "sica" it if a Thraex used one on you!

HOPLOMACHUS (The Greek Hoplite)

Wore a distinctive crested helmet with a visor, or face guard, carried a small round shield and brandished a deadly sharp spear. Excellent at bursting balloons after parties.

MURMILLO (The Roman)

Wore an arm guard on their sword arm, carried a large, rectangular wooden shield, and had a fancy bronze plumed-helmet. Armed with a *gladius*, the deadly sword of Roman soldiers. Best not to annoy.

RETIARIUS

Fought using a weighted net and a trident, which looks like an enormous fork. Didn't have a helmet. When not fighting they were good at catching fish and pretending to be a tiny person with a normal-sized fork.

SECUTOR

Weapons and armour were the same as the Murmillo, but their helmet enclosed the face completely – the visor had only two small eyeholes. Perfect for hiding a case of really bad spots!

FANCY THAT!

Occasionally, gladiators would fight so well that they would be seen as having fulfilled their contract to their owner and could be "set free". The decision was usually swayed by the opinion of the crowd, so a gladiator would have to be particularly impressive. When a gladiator was set free, they were presented with a wooden sword by an official or sometimes the emperor at a big ceremony. They then became a *rudiarius* (which has nothing to do with being rude) and could walk out of the arena as a free person.

RUDIARIUS (Free Person)

DIET

Remember that time your grandma made you a "special" meal? You know the one — she said it was something she used to eat when she was young.

It might have been meat but it also tasted strangely sweet. It **WOBBLED** like jelly when you prodded it with a fork and had something sprinkled on top that may have been dried **COW POO** or may have been something from a dusty jar at the back of the cupboard.

You might have forgotten that day. You've probably blocked it out of your memory to stop yourself having **NIGHTMARES**. But if you think your stomach has it bad, get a load of what the ancient Romans popped into their mouths!

SQUEAK!

Did you hear something?

No . . .

First things first: Romans had no potatoes, tomatoes or chocolate. So, if you're in the mood for fries, chips, crisps, ketchup or chocolate buttons, **GET OUTTA TOWN!** You can't have any.

However, if you fancy a delicious mouse then you're in for a treat! One dish recorded in ancient writing was dormice, served on a stick, cooked in honey and poppy seeds. You know something's gone weird when your **SNACK SQUEAKS**.

FANCY THAT!

Italy . . . the home of pasta: spaghetti, ravioli, penne, right? Wrong! Back in ancient Rome, you were very unlikely to find pasta on the menu. There may have been something a bit like lasagne, but the huge variety of pasta shapes that we love to MUNCH today hadn't been invented yet. So if you were after some ancient Roman macaroni cheese or spaghetti bolognese, you'd be fresh out of luck.

Although you couldn't have ketchup, there were other sauces available. For instance, a popular ingredient in Roman cooking was *garum*, a strong sauce made from . . . erm, fish entrails. That's right, the **OOZY GUTS** from inside a fish. But hey, the **STINKY STUFF** was probably used to disguise the flavour of meat that was starting to go off. So that's all right then.

Most ordinary people ate simple food rather than dormice. While the rich had kitchens and enslaved people to cook for them, the poor didn't have such things and would instead buy hot food from bars, called *thermopolia*, in the streets. Their diet would have mainly consisted of bread, beans, lentils and a little meat.

35

For wealthy Romans, the long evening meal was more of a social event than just a chance to eat. There would often be guests and entertainment between courses, with CLOWNS, dancers or POETRY READINGS.

Imagine finishing your CHICKEN NUGGETS and POTATO WAFFLES when a dude with a red nose and crazy hair suddenly leaps out and sprays you in the face with water from a fake flower. Not cool, Mr Clown. Not cool at all.

The rich dressed for dinner in an elegant Greek robe called a *synthesis*. What doesn't sound quite as classy is the fact that it was considered polite to BURP LOUDLY to show that you'd enjoyed your meal. Feel free to try it next time you have a special meal in a restaurant – your parents will be SO PROUD!

Why thank you! It's a new recipe for grilled sparrow I was trying out.

BUUUUUUUURRRRRRPPPPP!!!!!!

FANCY THAT!
A SKELETON was sometimes passed round at banquets to remind guests that life was short and should be enjoyed. It's similar to pass the parcel, but with fewer presents and more depressing reminders of death.

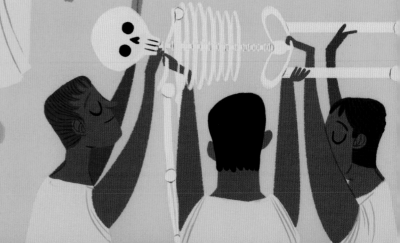

FANCY THAT!

Wealthy Romans used enslaved people to cook food, serve it and to provide entertainment during meals. There was even a servant called the "scissor" who would cut meat into bite-sized pieces for their masters. You can recreate the effect by using a pair of scissors to cut up a HOTDOG.

It looks like things really were quite different back then when it came to grub. Perhaps you're better sticking with **GRANDMA'S UFO** (Unidentified Foody Objects) after all.

Do you ever wish . . .

your mealtime choices could be more adventurous?

Fed up with fish fingers? Bored with beans? Well, spice up your life by getting some ancient Roman grub down your hatch.

While the first course could consist of jellyfish and eggs, the main course could have been ostrich, flamingo or, as previously mentioned, dormouse. Just think how many people you could feed with an ostrich . . . and what size of oven you'd need.

You might also like to nibble on pigs' udders with sea urchins. Or could we tempt you with some lip-smacking brain pâté with milk and eggs? Yes, of course you can have an extra-large helping!

While Emperor Augustus's advisor, Maecenas, made donkey meat a delicacy, that sounds positively delicious compared with the hard skin from an elephant's trunk, which the writer Pliny said was sought after by some.

On one occasion Emperor Vitellius served a huge dish of pike livers, pheasant and peacock brains and flamingo tongues with a side of lamprey slime. Something to remember when you're planning your next birthday party.

And don't worry – if the thought of all that weird food is making you feel queasy, Pliny wrote that eating an odd number of African snails marinated in wine or fish gut sauce was good for stomach upsets.

Still feeling peckish?

HEALTH AND MEDICINE

Unless you're called **WEIRDO MCBEARDO**, you are very unlikely to actually **ENJOY** going to visit a doctor.

It might be necessary, and you might feel better afterwards, but it's not the kind of thing you do as a **FUN HOBBY**.

Docs tend to poke you and prod you, shine lights in your earholes to see if you have a brain, peer up your nose with a **TELESCOPE**, make you say "aaaaahhhh" while pushing a lollipop stick down your throat and generally squeeze bits that make you scream "**OOOOYAH!**".

Say aaahh!

FANCY THAT!

Surgery in ancient Rome was usually for soldiers on the battlefields, but during the rule of Julius Caesar, it was also law that any pregnant mother who was dead or dying should be cut open to try to save the baby. Some people think this is where we get the word "caesarean" from.

But if you think you've got it bad, at least you don't have to **KISS MULES** or have a bath in **CABBAGEY WEE**. That's the kind of thing you might have come across in ancient Rome. More on that later . . .

The Romans were big on public health – but more when it came to keeping things clean. They understood that having sewers to take away the **SMELLY STUFF** and clean water to drink would improve people's wellbeing. But they weren't so bothered about medicine itself, preferring to use herbal remedies for illnesses instead.

The Greeks had developed many ideas about medicine, but the Romans didn't advance them, even when they took over Greece and Greek doctors came to Rome (often as enslaved people).

FENNEL

GARLIC

FENUGREEK

HERBAL REMEDIES

SAGE

ROSEMARY

Come in, come in. My name is Dr Allmypatientsdie and I'm going to be operating on you today. Wait! Come back!

The Greek doctor Archagathus was the first medic to come to Rome. At first people thought he was great, but then his way with a **BLADE** earned him the nickname "The Executioner"!

FANCY THAT!
Life was short in those days and for much of the population life expectancy wasn't much beyond 25 years old. War killed many men and childbirth killed many women. However, in one census some claimed to be as old as 140! Either they couldn't count or they were very WRINKLY FIBBERS!

WARNING!
If your doc is called anything like the Executioner, the Butcher or Big Jimmy Shakeyhands, FIND ANOTHER DOCTOR!

In the tough world of ancient Rome there was a general feeling that medicine was for **WEAKLINGS**, which is possibly one of the reasons they did not put great effort into developing it.

So if you've broken both legs or you've been run over by a herd of wild guinea pigs, stop lying around **MOANING** – and no, you're not getting a plaster!

But it hurts . . .

Don't be silly, now go out and play!

CATO THE ELDER

Although Roman medics were good at healing wounds and doing first aid – they had plenty of practice with soldiers and gladiators – some ideas about more complicated diseases could be a bit . . . errr, "out there".

For instance, historian Cato the Elder recommended that to make sure children grew up healthy they should be washed in the **WEE** of someone who had been eating mainly **CABBAGE**.

If you did that, you might be healthy, but you sure wouldn't have many friends . . .

CABBAGE

WEE BATH

FANCY THAT!

Gaius Marius — one of Rome's TOUGHEST military leaders — was the first person to have surgery without being tied down. You know things aren't going to be a jolly old giggle if the doc ties you to the bed before he gets his scalpel out. If you spot a rope beside the dentist's chair, run!

GAIUS MARIUS

It was said that strains and bruises could be treated with **WILD BOAR DUNG** gathered in spring and dried. Fresh dung could also be smeared on. Mind you, if you already stank of cabbage and wee, some **PIG POO** wasn't going to make much difference.

If you had a face full of spots, some Roman doctors would prescribe taking a bath in oil and sour cheese to get rid of them. Mmmm, **GROSS** and **STINKY**! No pimples, but you **REEK** of **STILTON!** Thanks, but no thanks, Doc! If that didn't work, you could always try rubbing your skin with crocodile meat and Cyprus oil. At last – a use for all that spare croc meat you've got lying around . . .

In ancient Rome, there were also plenty of strange "cures" connected with our furry, feathered or CREEPY-CRAWLY friends.

According to Pliny, cobwebs were used to stop bleeding from fractured **SKULLS** while bleeding on the brain was treated with the blood and fat of geese and ducks.

Well, I suppose it's worth a try . . .

GOOSE BLOOD

DUCK FAT

Kissing a mule's nose was said to stop sneezing and hiccups, and if you were stung by a **SCORPION**, whispering in a donkey's ear would mean that the pain was immediately transferred to the donkey. It's not clear if whispering in a scorpion's ear would help if you were bitten by a donkey, but anything's worth a try.

If you had a headache, one suggested cure was to **SOAK A CHAMELEON IN WINE**, and then to sprinkle the wine on your head. If that didn't do the trick, you could see if you could find an elephant to touch you on the head with its trunk, and hope that it sneezed. Hmmm . . . sore head or face full of **GROSS ELEPHANT BOGIES?** On second thoughts, the aching noggin doesn't feel that bad after all, thanks.

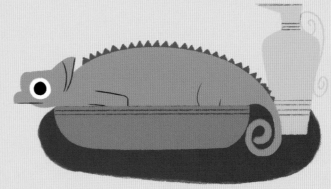

By and large it seems that even if you're not keen on being prodded at the docs these days, it sure beats being covered in poop, pee, trunk gunk or **SNOGGING MULES!**

Do you ever wish . . . your medicine was more magical?

There are very few people who like the taste of medicine, which usually resembles a mixture of earwax and paint. Perhaps you'd prefer it if pharmacists adopted the more magical approach that some ancient Romans favoured. These were particularly popular when performed by Egyptian priests, who were seen as the best "magicians".

Then you could choose from some of the following "alternative" remedies:
• the longest tooth of a black dog
• a wasp caught in the left hand and attached under the patient's chin
• a viper's severed head
• a lizard's right eye wrapped in goat skin

Try asking your doc for one of those next time you're feeling poorly. We're sure they'll have a big bag of wasps and lizards' eyes hidden in their desk drawer, just in case.

If they don't, simply grab some paper and a pen. One ancient Roman medical textbook has the following cure for fever: write abracadabra on a piece of paper then roll it up and wear it round the neck in an amulet. The word has to be written like this to work:

ABRACADABRA
ABRACADAB
ABRACADA
ABRACAD
ABRACA
ABRAC
ABRA
ABR
AB

You'll be better before you know it! (Maybe.)

EMPERORS BEHAVING BADLY

So, the head teacher in your school. Possibly an alien? Or maybe some kind of ZOMBIE-VAMPIRE-WEREWOLF mash-up? What do you reckon?

Definitely some kind of **MONSTER**, that's for sure.

That's the only way to explain what a **TYRANT** they are! What with all the making you do schoolwork and wear school uniform and not ride **MOTORBIKES** in the corridors and stuff.

But if you think you've got it bad, at least the guy in charge isn't prone to feeding you to **WILD ANIMALS**, burning down your town or being nasty to giraffes.

While some of the Roman emperors were regarded as wise, brave or fair – such as Marcus Aurelius or Augustus – some have gone down in history as being cruel, brutal . . . or just **DOWNRIGHT WEIRD**.

Three of the most infamous were Caligula, Nero and Commodus. You would **DEFINITELY** do your schoolwork if any of these guys told you to.

COMMODUS

CALIGULA

NERO

Do you ever wish . . . something BIG would happen in your neighbourhood?

Do you think your town should be renamed Dullsville? Is the most exciting thing that happens around your way open day at the Paperclip Museum?

Well how about a volcano! That would liven things up a bit, wouldn't it?

Be careful what you wish for. Back in AD 79, the Roman towns of Pompeii and Herculaneum were destroyed when Mount Vesuvius erupted on a sunny summer afternoon.

Burning ash rained down on the towns, burying everything up to four metres (13 feet) deep and trapping the residents where they cowered. The ashes hardened around the bodies of those who died, eventually creating hollow "moulds" of their original shapes. The shapes of people of all ages and animals, including a dog, have been discovered.

They were frozen in time by the dust, and although it is not known exactly how many people died, it's assumed that the remains of the 1,500 people that have so far been uncovered by archaeologists are just a fraction of the total number.

Anyone fancy a trip to the Paperclip Museum?

Kids in ancient Rome would have known who the emperor was, especially if they had a reputation for being FEARSOME or unpredictable.

CALIGULA began his reign in AD 37 in a positive way, but after an unidentified illness he REALLY went off the rails.

For a start, he promised to make his favourite horse, Incitatus, a consul – one of the most important political officials in ancient Rome. While that was a bit odd, on another occasion he ordered his guards to throw an entire section of the audience at a games into the arena to be EATEN by wild beasts because there were no prisoners to be used and he was BORED.

It was also claimed he declared war on the sea. Which is a bit like trying to punch the sky or have an argument with OUTER SPACE.

INCITATUS

Right! That's it! If you make my knees wet one more time, you are FOR it! And you're next, sand, so you can stop giggling.

Caligula's nephew, **NERO**, carried on his uncle's reputation for general **NAUGHTINESS**.

It was said at the time that he started the Great Fire of Rome in AD 64 on purpose (though that is debated). The fire is reported to have burned for over a week and destroyed or badly damaged much of the city.

HMMM...

Try this cake, it's really *wood* . . . I mean good!

The Roman historian Suetonius wrote that Nero started the fire because he wanted the space to build his Golden House, a massive palace that included a 30-meter-tall statue of himself called the Colossus of Nero. He also killed several members of his own family, including his own mother. Which is just **RUDE**.

FANCY THAT!

The very strange emperor Elagabalus came to power when he was barely 14 years old. Among the less unpleasant things he was said to have done was feed dinner guests food made of wax, wood, pottery and other things that JUST AREN'T FOOD, while he ate a real banquet. What a cheeky little prankster!

47

Later on came a really bad lad called COMMODUS. Look away now if you have a soft spot for giraffes.

Commodus had a passion for gladiatorial combat and would often fight in the arena himself alongside, or more frequently *against*, the gladiators. Funnily enough he always "won".

He even charged the city **ONE MILLION** *sesterces* for each appearance. That's like your head teacher demanding he plays football for the school team, threatening to give **EVERYONE LINES** if they stop him scoring, and then charging everyone megabucks for the privilege!

One of the many horrible things cruel Commodus enjoyed was killing wild animals in the arena, which made the people of Rome grow to **HATE** him. He once slew 100 lions in a single day, and if that wasn't enough, he also killed a defenceless giraffe and some terrified elephants, much to the justifiable **DISGUST** of the spectators.

Not surprisingly, all of these **HORRID** characters met a **GRISLY END**. Caligula was murdered by his own guards; Nero was declared an enemy of the state – so he ran away and then killed himself; and Commodus was strangled in his bath by an assassin sent by his political enemies (who also happened to love giraffes).

So next time you get a telling off for playing the fool in school, just be thankful your head teacher isn't a Roman emperor.

FANCY THAT!
When he was 11 years old Commodus complained that his bath water was too cold and ordered the man responsible to be thrown into the furnace! A sheepskin was burned instead so the cruel boy would think the deed had been done. Talk about overreacting!

ANCIENT ROMAN GODS

Why are people ALWAYS telling you what to do? What IS their problem? Why can't they mind their own beeswax? Huh?

There's your mum ordering you to dismantle the **STINKY SOCK MOUNTAIN** from the corner of your bedroom, your dad warning you to stop picking your nose with your fork at the dinner table, and your teacher telling you to wake up when you were trying to have a little **SNOOZE** during maths.

But if you think you've got it bad with a handful of grown ups on your case all the time, at least you don't have **LOADS OF GODS** keeping an eye on you, too.

In ancient Rome, they didn't have just one **BIG CHEESE** in the sky – they had a whole bunch of them!

Here are some of the most important:

JUPITER was the most important god – he was god of the sky. He was also the god of thunder, so if you're scared of the rumbly stuff, blame ol' Jupe.

FANCY THAT!

Most of the ancient Roman gods and goddesses were actually ancient Greek gods and goddesses . . . but with sparkly new Roman names.

GREEK	ROMAN
Zeus	Jupiter
Cronus	Saturn
Hera	Juno
Poseidon	Neptune
Athena	Minerva
Ares	Mars
Aphrodite	Venus

SATURN was once the king of the gods until his son Jupiter took his place. Saturn was the god of seed-sowing, which makes him sound a bit like a very powerful gardener.

JUNO was Jupiter's wife and she looked after women. She is often shown armed with a weapon and wearing a goatskin cloak, so best not to mess with her. Especially if you're a goat.

NEPTUNE was the god of the sea. His temper was violent and the ancient Romans thought he caused earthquakes when he was angry. Best not to steal his sandals when he's not looking!

MINERVA was the goddess of wisdom, and was therefore handy to know when it came to doing homework.

MARS was not a chocolate bar but the god of war, which isn't nearly as good. Given the choice between chocolate and war, **ALWAYS** choose chocolate.

VENUS was the goddess of love. Like many of the Roman gods, her name was given to one of the planets in our solar system.

If you think that's A LOT of gods, think again! People from throughout the Roman Empire worshipped HUNDREDS of different gods and goddesses. They were usually depicted in human form, but much larger.

I'm going to have to send these trousers back. They're size XL, but I need an XXXXXXXXXXXXXXXXXXXXXXXL.

Should've gone to Gods 'R' Us, mate.

As you would expect, there were gods who protected the home, gods of healing, gods of farming, gods of jelly beans, gods of baseball caps . . . and errr, gods of making stuff up.

There were also many minor gods and goddesses, some whom weren't very glamorous. Verminus was the protector of cattle, Runcina was goddess of weeding (and lawn mowing!), and Stercutus was the god of faeces (yup, the god of **POO**), whose job was to teach people about **MANURE SPREADING**. Hopefully not with a personal demonstration.

VERMINIUS

STERCUTUS

They might seem boring today, but all these things were incredibly important in ancient times – in fact, they could be a matter of **LIFE AND DEATH**. If your crops failed because the manure you spread wasn't rich enough to fertilise the soil, or your plants were choked with weeds, you would be looking at a long, hungry winter (and wishing you'd spent a lot more time worshipping Runcina and Stercutus).

The Romans even had a festival every year for the goddess Furrina*. . . even though everyone in ancient Rome had forgotten why she was actually a goddess! Best worship her just in case she's the goddess of something **REALLY COOL!**

> Give me an "F"!

> Give me a "U"!

> Bless us, Furrina, and grant us, er . . . whatever it is you grant . . .

*She was actually the goddess of bubbling springs, not bad as ancient Roman god jobs go!

FANCY THAT!

The chief priest of Jupiter had many privileges but also some rather odd rules about what he couldn't do. He could not leave Rome for a night, touch or mention dogs, beans or ivy, or be NAKED outdoors. So consider yourself lucky that you can do all of those things (apart from the last one, hopefully).

The Romans FEARED and respected their gods and would pray and make offerings and sacrifices.

WARNING!

Do not attempt to conduct your own sacrifices. EVER! If you really must give it a go, stick to cutting a sausage in half or poking a chicken nugget with a fork.

Everything from coins, jewellery and silver statues, to food and drink was offered to the gods, and animal **SACRIFICES** were common.

At one end of the scale a bird might be sacrificed – but at the other end, a whole herd of cattle could be offered if you **REALLY** wanted to impress a god! Sacrificing a mosquito probably wouldn't get you much in the way of favours from the big guys and gals in the clouds, though.

Before sacrificing a large animal, a priest would bathe and put on ceremonial robes. Male animals were sacrificed for gods, and female animals for goddesses. The animals were also given a wash and decorated with ribbons and embroidered blankets, and sometimes their horns (if they had any) were painted with gold. To be honest, looking simply **FABULOUS** probably didn't make them feel a whole lot better, due to the whole "about to be sacrificed" thing.

With so many gods to keep happy back then, you'd have to be careful not to upset one god by spending too much time worshipping another! Sounds EXHAUSTING. At least you don't have to sacrifice a cow to please your teacher!

FANCY THAT!

Sometimes animal-shaped cakes were used as offerings to the gods instead of sacrificing an animal. That sound you can hear is a Roman god chomping a sheep-shaped cake. That other sound is a sheep breathing a sigh of relief.

Do you ever wish . . .
you could predict the future?

Wouldn't it be useful to be able to know when bad or good things were going to happen – like you were about to stand on a Lego brick in the dark, or find a sweet you thought you'd lost a month ago down the back of the sofa?

In ancient Rome, they believed in omens, symbols and magical curses.

After an animal was killed in a sacrifice to the gods, its inner organs were removed so that priests could study them. They would read the gods' will from the shape of the liver, for example. If it was deformed it was thought to be a bad omen. You can try doing the same thing with a sausage. Straight sausage = good; wonky sausage = bad.

There were other things which suggested a positive or negative response from the gods. The way sacred chickens ate, for example, showed whether or not the gods approved of a plan.

Symbols and superstitions were everywhere in ancient Rome. Good and bad signs included:

OWLS – may signal disaster
SOUND OF BELLS – thought to ease childbirth
BEES – sacred messengers of the gods and symbols of good luck
EAGLES – said to bring thunderstorms

So always be polite to a bee, and if you hear an owl hoot, hide under your bed.

FUN AND GAMES

We all need a little bit of fun in our lives. Games! Sports! Hobbies! What do YOU do for enjoyment and relaxation?

Perhaps you collect belly button fluff in jam jars? Or take your pet earwig on long walks in the woods?

Or are you an **ACE** at the little-known sport of **CHEESEPOODLE?** You know the one – you roll up tiny balls of cheddar and flick them at a poodle? The more balls it catches in its mouth, the more points you get. **THAT'S CHEESEPOODLE!**

Actually, if those **WEIRD** pastimes are all you've got to keep you busy, perhaps you **DO** have it bad! For all the **BRUTAL, UNPLEASANT AND STRANGE** things going on in ancient Rome, the folk back then still knew how to enjoy themselves.

One of the most popular forms of entertainment was chariot racing.

If you love football today, it was probably on the same level as that – and people got just as **PASSIONATE** about their teams as you do about yours. Maybe a little more so . . .

In Rome, the four chariot racing teams were the Blues, Greens, Reds and Whites — nice and simple. But sometimes the rival fans got into fights with each other. In the city of Constantinople (which is now in modern-day Turkey, but was part of the Roman Empire back in AD 532) fighting between the Blues and the Greens spiralled into a riot in which both teams joined forces to try and overthrow the emperor. Nearly half of the city was **BURNED OR DESTROYED** and tens of thousands of people were killed! Whoops. You don't get that sort of behaviour in Cheesepoodle!

The Circus Maximus, where chariot racing took place in Rome, was the largest venue in the city. It held up to 250,000 people! So it was a **BIG DEAL**.

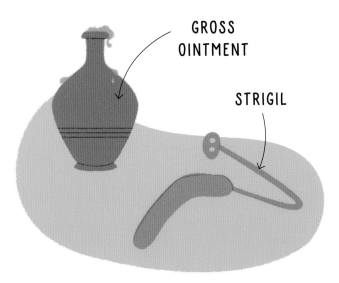

GROSS OINTMENT

STRIGIL

FANCY THAT!

The combination of sweat, dirt and olive oil scraped with a *strigil* from the bodies of top athletes was sometimes sold to the public for huge prices. It was used in ointments to cure ailments. Why not try selling a tub of your grubby sweat for big bucks? GOOD LUCK!

Of course, not everyone was a fan of loud, ROUGH-AND-TUMBLE sports.
Some preferred quieter pursuits.

Swimming in the River Tiber was one of the favourite activities of Roman children, and boys also enjoyed learning to ride horses – though not at the same time. Swimming while riding a horse is **NOT** to be encouraged – especially at your local public pool.

FANCY THAT!

Ancient Roman ball games played outside could be dangerous. One legal case recorded how a barber was shaving a man's neck with a razor when he was hit by a ball . . . with EXTREMELY bloody results. That would have been one AAAWKWAAARD request to get the ball back!

Roman children were also keen on flying kites, ball games, playing at being soldiers or gladiators with wooden swords, rolling hoops made from pieces of metal, playing with toy chariots or centaurs with wheels that were pulled along on a string or with a stick, and playing with dolls.

So nothing much has changed in thousands of years. Apart from the metal hoop thing. The Romans can keep that, thanks.

Board games were also an option. Ancient Romans played games such as dice, knucklebones (which is like jacks), Roman chess, tic-tac-toe and Roman backgammon.

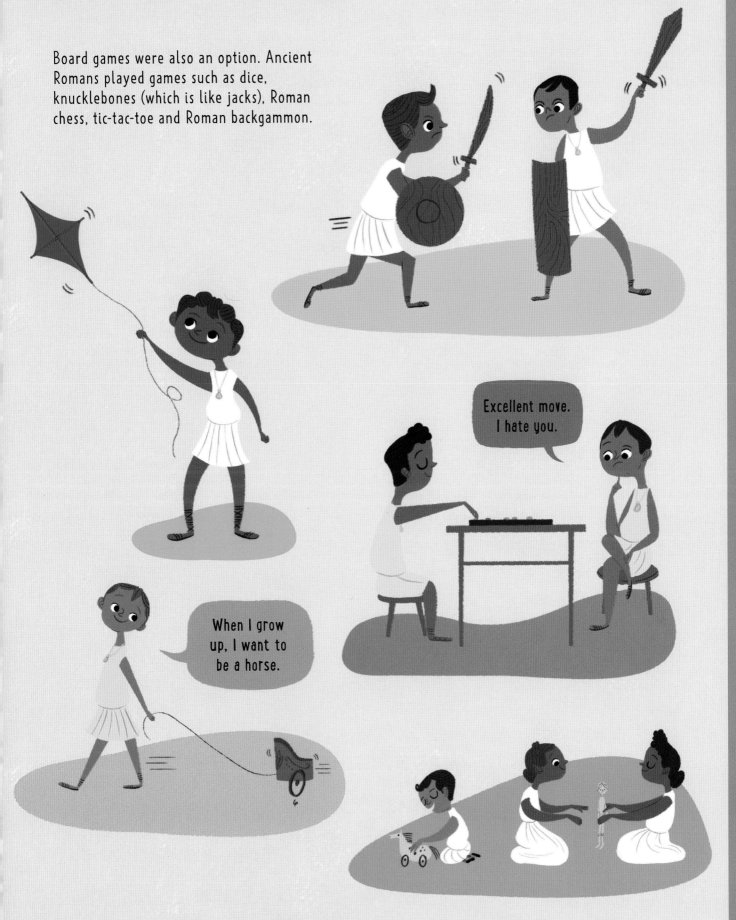

All in all, while life could be a **LOT** tougher then than it is now, when it came to enjoying themselves there wasn't much difference between the ancient Romans and us.

We all just want a little bit of **FUN** in our lives.

59

STILL THINK YOU'VE GOT IT BAD?

So that's it for our whistle-stop tour of ancient Rome and all the SMELLY, DIRTY, WEIRD and downright NASTY things that went on back in the days of emperors, gladiators and POO SPONGES on sticks.

Of course, now you've seen the reality of life back then, you can't STILL believe you have it bad nowadays, can you?

This is the part where you're meant to shout: "NO WAY!" But you seem awfully quiet right now. So let's just have a quick recap of the evidence . . .

Are you finished with that?

It's MY turn to play with Cornelia!

Example 1: Nowadays you might see a bad tackle at a football match that makes you go: "Ooooo, I bet that stung." Back then you might watch someone be poked to death with a giant fork and turned into **BEAR-FOOD**.

Example 2: Nowadays if you get head lice, it's treated with lotion and a good comb. Back then? A noggin-full of **GOAT POO!**

Example 3: Nowadays you might order a burger and fries at a fast food joint. Back then you'd end up with a **McUDDER** and a side-order of **BRAIN SPREAD**.

More poo, please!

We're all out of brain burgers for today!

So before you start rolling around dramatically on the ground screaming: **"IT'S SO UNFAIR! I HAVE IT SOOOOOOO BAD!"** here is the news: you really don't!

GLOSSARY

Your tiny brainbox must be BURSTING at the seams (do brainboxes have seams?) with all the fabulous facts you've just read about those Roman dudes from ancient times.

From SNEEZING ELEPHANTS and cakes made of wood to jellyfish snacks and GOLDEN POOP POTS, it's been quite a ride! But if you reckon you can squeeze a few little itty-bitty wafer thin facts into that overloaded coconut of yours without it going "BOOM", then here you go . . .

AMULET

Amulets were charms or pouches that were worn somewhere on the body — often around the neck. It was believed they had magical powers to protect the wearer. Not to be confused with a HAMulet, which is a rasher of bacon worn round the neck. It isn't magic.

BEESWAX

Bees produce flakes of wax which they chew until it becomes soft so they can make their honeycombs from it. It can be used to make candles or, in the Romans' case, to make a wax surface to write on. The sad thing is bees don't need candles and can't write, so will never get to use these things.

CHARIOTEERS

Charioteers drove chariots. Chariot racing was one of the most popular, but also most dangerous, sports. Drivers and horses often suffered serious injury and even death — the life expectancy of a charioteer was only 22! Best sticking to table tennis!

CONSUL

A consul was the most important elected political official in ancient Rome. Their responsibilities included choosing senators (who helped make the rules), making sure the government worked properly and directing the army (who often got lost! Only kidding).

DORMOUSE

There is more than one type of dormouse, and the one the Romans ate is called the Edible Dormouse. It's the largest of all dormice, and looks like a cross between a mouse and a squirrel. If they wanted to avoid being chomped, they should probably have considered changing their name.

GLADIATOR SCHOOL

Gladiators trained in schools. They lived in small cells, arranged around a central practice arena. Discipline could be very brutal . . . sometimes even deadly. If you think your school is strict, at least you don't use REAL SWORDS in P.E.

INSULA

An *insula* was an apartment block. Most of the middle class and poorer people in cities lived in this kind of building. Insula was Latin for "island", although given that the buildings were prone to catching fire or collapsing they perhaps should have been renamed "insulaaaarrrrggghhh!".

LARES

Lares were the spirits of dead ancestors. Daily prayers and offerings were made to the lares so they would look after the house. Every home had a *lalarium* where their statuettes were kept. Not to be confused with a *LOLarium*, which was a shrine to the god of hilarious jokes.

LAUREL WREATH

A laurel wreath was a crown of leaves that was used in ancient Rome to mark a successful commander during his triumph (a parade) after a victory in battle. You can recreate the look by taping a small shrub to your hat next time you win at Monopoly.

MARK ANTONY

Mark Antony was a Roman general who served under famous Roman leader Julius Caesar. He was in love with Cleopatra, queen of Egypt, and Rome declared him a traitor during a civil war in 31 BC. He didn't have a happy ending. In fact, it was a dead end . . .

PHILOSOPHY

This is the use of thinking and reason to try to understand the world, why we exist and things like morals and judgement. It's the kind of thing that can make your noggin throb, but also makes it strong — like weightlifting for your brain.

PLINY THE ELDER

A famous writer and naval officer, Pliny wrote a book called *Natural Histories*, which was like an encyclopaedia. He suffocated from fumes when Mount Vesuvius erupted as he sailed his ship to the area to try to save people. Lesson learned: do not sail into big clouds of smoke caused by erupting volcanoes.

RIVER TIBER

The second longest river in what is now Italy. According to legend, the city of Rome was founded in 753 BC on the banks of the Tiber by Rome's founders, the twin brothers Romulus and Remus, who were cared for by a she-wolf called Lupa. That must have made for an interesting parents' evening at school.

SESTERTII/SESTERTIUS

An ancient Roman coin, worth between two-and-a-half and four *asses*. No, it had nothing to do with donkeys! An *as* was a bronze coin, while a *denarius* was silver. Do not ask for an ass (or a donkey) as pocket money.

STRIGIL

A curved blade used to scrape sweat and dirt from the skin in a bath or after exercise. Unless you're EXTREMELY grubby, you'll probably manage with a sponge.

STYLUS

A stylus looks a bit like a thick, blunt nail. They were made from materials such as metal, bone or ivory and used to write in the wax on tablets. It might not sound very high-tech but at least a stylus can't burst and leak all over your schoolbag.

TALI

In ancient Rome, the game of knucklebones was called *tali* and involved bones being thrown in the air and caught in various ways. And they weren't really knuckles — they were the *astragalus*, a bone in the ankle of a sheep. Which was baaaaa-d news for sheep.

INDEX